PRAISE FOR

"Jalen Eutsey's *Bubble Gum Stadium* captures the nostalgia of witness that is growing up in Miami—where the city dons the jerseys of Black boys made legend, and t-shirts archive loved ones. In this suite of everyday survivals, Eutsey allows the reader to witness the spectacle of becoming that is Black boyhood. This chapbook wonders, dreams, and buzzes like the bass of a lowrider in a parade. Here, beauty and trauma are equidistant and the mundane is made canonical."

– Christell Victoria Roach, Emmy-Nominated Writer & Spoken Word Artist

"*Bubble Gum Stadium* is a trip. Jalen Eutsey's study of place, race, and recollection transports us through the vibrant ballfields, parks, streets, and homes of South Florida's West Perrine. Varied in their forms and vivid in their music, his poems traverse that richly textured landscape on a journey from adolescent naiveté into canny adulthood. Eutsey's is a keen and singular American perspective, this is a rich and heartfelt debut, and I am just plain grateful to go along on its memorable ride."

– Jaswinder Bolina, *English as a Second Language and Other Poems*

"With clarity of attention and such a supple ease, Jalen Eutsey's poems conjure home and its generations. Here we are in that lush reverberation of Black aliveness out of which he emerges and which he so stunningly attends. Exact, ruminative, skillful. *Bubble Gum Stadium* is a slim and gorgeous glimpse of Eutsey's exquisite, singular sound."

– aracelis girmay, *the black maria*

BUBBLE GUM STADIUM

BUBBLE GUM STADIUM

poems by

Jalen Eutsey

Button Publishing Inc.
Minneapolis
2025

BUBBLE GUM STADIUM
POETRY
AUTHOR: Jalen Eutsey
COVER DESIGN: Victoria Alvarez

ALL RIGHTS RESERVED

© 2025 by Jalen Eutsey

Published by Button Poetry
Minneapolis, MN 55418 | http://www.buttonpoetry.com

Manufactured in the United States of America
PRINT ISBN: 978-1-63834-204-5
EBOOK ISBN: 978-1-63834-131-4

First printing

TABLE OF CONTENTS

3	WEST PERRINE, FLORIDA
5	HOUSE GUESTS
7	SONNET
8	SONNET
9	BOYHOOD: A SHOT LIST
11	SUMMER
12	CINEMA VERITÉ
13	RAINBOW CITY
15	SONNET
16	SNUFF
18	FOOT RACE
19	FIELD SERVICE
20	SURPRISE VISIT
22	F-STOP
25	TO MY CARING AND WORRIED MOTHER:
27	DÉGRINGOLADE
28	SONNET
29	THE COLOSSUS OF MIAMI
30	WEST PERRINE PARK (THE BIG PARK)
32	UNSENT LETTER TO MY LITTLE COUSIN
33	SONNET
34	MOTHER'S VISIT
39	ACKNOWLEDGMENTS
43	ABOUT THE AUTHOR
45	AUTHOR BOOK RECOMMENDATIONS
49	CREDITS

BUBBLE GUM STADIUM

...intimate land condemned to amnesia

—Eduardo Galeano

WEST PERRINE, FLORIDA

Bare, bird-chested boys play touch
football in the street, reenact
WrestleMania in the fenced-in front yard.

When an errant pass rocks a mailbox
the whole block takes off running.

After the game that never ends
is paused, a swarm of sweaty boys
meander to the corner store
to buy a pickled egg, a hot sausage.

At Galvez and B Seafood
they call the woman working
behind the counter *Mami*
and order conch-fritters
with french fries, squeeze
lemon juice over the conch,
crisscrossing ketchup
and mustard over the juice.

Here, in this cut-out
between Hemingway's
Key West home
and Jenkins' *Moonlight*,
gunfire dapples
the far-off night.

One day, a man
in a black Mercedes
will inch up
alongside
and ask:

You working?
Nah.
You wanna work?
Nah.

HOUSE GUESTS

My mother has two house guests.
Her house guests, two children,
make a mess of the living room, make
a brimming biome of an oriental red—
hand-tufted, wool, and littered with animals:
minuscule, plush, bean-filled, and breaking.

The older child is a sweet, sensitive,
clever little nightmare. She is afraid
of the dark and worships her father.
They talk on the phone for hours.
She is bright and deceitful
like an Orchid Mantis.

The younger one puts her hand out,
opening and closing it
whenever she sees food. *Gimme*
says the soft palm, the short fingers.
Gimme says the panting dog
scratching at a dust-brown bowl,
hard plastic and empty.

My mother
has two house guests
not unlike plants or bees,
never far from sunlight
and honey.

There is a drawer full
of juice pouches.
Below them, different
bottles with different caps,
a jar of Enfamil.

Beneath the brown sectional
and at my mother's feet,
a small cardboard staircase,
nearly weightless, made
for a small dog with a history
of knee problems.

Above the staircase, the dog,
smooth, sheeny, and brown,
curls up like a waxing gibbous
with pointy ears, sleeping.

SONNET

Disease spins eddies in the blood
of your kin and bullets do what they will
in the dark. Yet the repass still smells
of fried catfish and ham hocks—someone must
make a run for more hot sauce. In the dream
that is memoir, you died before a king
tide swept through the city and reshaped coast-
line and inland escape without bias,
before anyone could solve the brutal
mystery of blue—you never gave Maggie
Nelson the time of day. What about gray—
the brain's subtle decay, another coast
left lifeless, left longing in rank silence.

SONNET

>For Biker Boy Will

How could America ever love you?
She misunderstands your fresh-pressed white T,
the gaudy ticking gold on your left wrist,
the swim trunks and fitted, the retro J's
gracing the grimy pink-red outside courts.
She don't know what to do with all your swagger
and braggadocious bluster, the gum-flapping
wolf—pronounced *woof*—tickets. You said,
the losing team's son aint gon eat tonight.
You said the game was for five racks.
You could lie your ass off.
You said, *this shit is really really hard.*
But of course, there is a mother's protection—
my old girl kept me in the house, and I thank her for that.

BOYHOOD: A SHOT LIST

1. Unmoving morning
   fog & waveless water—
   sly, artful alligators
   hunting the quivering
   bass hooked at the end
   of my rod & hanging
   below a trafficless bridge

2. The mangled line
   on the way to mastery

3. Heavy tome of quotes
   jostling beneath the passenger seat
   of my father's red F-150

4. The east/west divider
   of a busway, placed atop
   the ghost of a railroad
   where the long ride out
   the neighborhood began

5. Fish & grits, *dizzy biscuits*,
   farmer's tans & Fuddruckers—
   my *dark* neck in summer

6. Sickness & holistic healing—
   minced onions in my socks,
   sliced onions on my chest,
   foot baths, echinacea, &
   reflexology's deep tissue
   massage

7. The rough skin
   of a lychee
   & a laundry list
   of unattended
   quinceañeras

8. Asthma attacks, pre-sweetened
   espresso, & retro glass-block
   windows

9. The unnatural lean
   to my cousin's mouth
   when he got out

10. Fickle bouncers
    holding my fate
    in their hands
    like the last match
    hissing in the breeze
    & the wind wicked
    playful

SUMMER

Some kids lit fireworks
in the big tree in the big park,
hollowed out the trunk
of a state treasure.

Some kids, they say,
started a mattress fire
in the little park,
charred the jungle gym.

Three shirtless boys
backflip on the narrow
balance beam head
of a cracked, pink wall—

painting the space
between oak leaves
and air with their
rich luminescence.

CINEMA VERITÉ

I never forgot
the stillness
in the street
after the small mob
rode off
on bikes
like little children,
the hero
writhing
in the center
of the frame.

I live
for the frame:
an open ocean
baptism, rusted
triangles of sky,
silent
tower speakers
in a bed
of branches.

An empty
Hot Cheeto bag
caught in
crab grass
flapping
like a flag
in wind.

RAINBOW CITY

Three shirtless boys tiptoe
the high wire of a wall, faces
shadowed by a willow.

They teeter atop a tightrope,
a bed of dew-wet blades
beneath.

Three shirtless boys dance
on the white-trimmed lip,
nearing the exactness needed to fly.

They trickle along the wall
like scurrying blue crabs,
love-sick for the sea.

Propped atop this ripe
peach border, they dangle
their legs over the ledge

as their sweat-slick skin
beams above passing cars.
I drive by. Blink them miniature.

They play lookout for no one.
They float above the street
thirsting for a quarter water.

They talk about chocolate
cities and the scent
of a beach rarely seen.

They kick their heels
against a pastel past, no better
than the blackened present.

SONNET

The story always starts with slaves,
a sucked-up swamp, some ill-placed railway,
and generations worth of loot overstuffed
into bags and bull-knotted around
the ankles of the not-yet-dead. Later,
the capital starts to play its bloody
melody. Song of Solomon, your choice
book in the good word. There was a poet
deep inside you when you said, *you got to
bring yours to get mine*, when you curved *orange*
and *road*, and planned a grandchild's whooping.
Like the perfect bend of a switch, the turn
takes time to master. We kept our promise.
This sonnet is the sole box you'll sleep in.

SNUFF

My daddy packed a pinch of Skoal Mint
sexier than most things I've seen women do.

Once, he offered me and my adolescent tongue
a taste out of some old-school, parochial sense

of education—let the rod of experience thunder
loud and profound, where the lips might only

whisper unintentional invitations. Like the clued-in
June bug I was, I heard alarm bells blaring behind

my eyes, blind with admiration. I decided,
simply, to watch and marvel at the way my daddy

carried himself with so much swagger. The way
he kept a Diet Pepsi bottle in his back pocket

stuffed with paper towels and dip spit—as cool
as the coldest mink on the coat rack. I settled

for a different red and black map of imitation—
a can of Jack Link's Beef Chew. Fattened my lip

with the finely ground meat and juice, slipped
the faux snuff into the back pocket of my baseball pants

with scandalous intent, as if it was the plastic foil O
of a condom wrapper, leaning into my little secret,

the lead-up to my big joke, my wry smile and reveal.
My daddy's vice as beautiful as a well-made blade—

the astringent mint making Jean's Nicot(ine) sing,
setting the gums ablaze. He quit and un-quit

and I learned what you can and can't make of a man.
But one day, on the red clay of black Miami,

where the diamonds go mostly unused,
I got bit by a wasp while fielding groundballs.

My father took the wet contents of his bottom lip
and pressed it to the bite, stemming the pain and swelling.

I got to return to one of baseball's cherished
rhythmic routines—catch, step, and pitch it to first.

FOOT RACE

When I dusted the other black boy in the foot race, I tried to do it with a tender panache. He took a good look at me and I him. He saw the bleach-perfumed house and the couplet of germaphobe matriarchs. He could see the expensive wood bats stacked in the corner of my closet—Marucci, Old Hickory, Sam. I could see he was no athlete by the way he carried himself or didn't. I knew he wasn't running miles on beaches or over bridges. I could see his hands hadn't been ripped open then calloused from thousands of swings. He had no small mound on the inside of his lip where the red, stitched seams of a baseball had stolen a kiss, bloodied up a black and teal uniform. I told him I was tired, maybe some other time, I said. When the race was over, he was still singing the same tune, talking some big talk about luck, a bad break out of the imaginary blocks, the unevenness of the outfield grass behind second base, and I loved him for it.

FIELD SERVICE

As a boy, I went door to door
with my mother and grandmother.
At first, I only knocked, played
my part as mascot.

My mother, thinner then
before three knee surgeries,
and my grandmother, always
wearing her straw hat—they did
the talking when I was a boy.

My mother, firm and intimidating,
greeted every open door
with a wide smile and two magazines—
Watchtower and *Awake*.

I remember the clip-on ties,
penny loafers, and small leather
briefcase my mother bought
so I could look the part.

I can't quite remember when I first
started to speak at the door—
wave my hand at the homeowners.
We bring you good news, I must've said.

SURPRISE VISIT

Mangoes ripening in a wicker basket—
tough and green, you could skin them
and eat them with salt. In the oven,
the softening flesh of salmon,
waiting to be pulled out and served
with yellow grits and butter. My mother
was away when two visitors came knocking.

What I can describe is the powder blue
chalk-outlined hopscotch box, beginning
with your first step off the fading beige
front porch so that you could jump or drop
into play the way you might slip into a riff
of your grandaddy's country twang and wisdom.

What I can describe is the flaking
floral porch column and brown coir
welcome mat—rough to the touch
of bare feet or, if by some cruelty,
the sensitive skin of the cheek.

My cousin lived in the fenced-in house
across the street before he slept on our couch.
His mother lived next door in a seaweed green
duplex with a small backyard and a metal line
used to air-dry damp clothes. She was alive
when the visitors came, or she wasn't.

All I have is one good shoulder, two good feet,
and memory: the elementary school field trip
where I eased out to the bathroom then quenched
my thirst at the water cooler while the other kids
cheesed and marveled at the fingerprinting process.
I think they used black ink, black like these visitors' uniforms.

I tell these men, the man they seek
never lived here, has left no valuables,
or products, no secrets, but the mystery
of his brief life. When they demanded
a more senior presence, my grandmother
cracked the door a little wider and spoke
with the detachment of a disembodied voice:

We do not speak to the dead, it's against our beliefs.
We do not trifle with ghosts, even ones we birthed.

F-STOP

I saw a man walking
with a monopod in his left hand,
camera in his right.

His wrist tucked into
the string at the top
of the rubber hand grip.

The monopod twisting
and swaying with the rhythm
of his stride.

There was a soccer game
going on in the stadium
behind me. Faint cheers

rose and fell
as we passed each other.
I blinked and the monopod

was a nightstick. I blinked
and tasted danger, remembered
the cost of existence

in the only body
I have blessed with breath.
I blinked and saw a monopod,

saw all the pictures
I wouldn't take:
my firstborn

naked in a bathtub
with floaties on.
The woman of my dreams

in jeans and unflattering glasses
standing at the edge
of the Grand Canyon.

I blinked and saw
a picture I'd never see again,
pilfered

from my middle school
Myspace,
thin adolescent body,

toothy smile
blemished by twisted
fingers, a gesturing hand.

I blinked and thought
of last night's party,
the way I sat

on the black vinyl couch
and the respectable friends
who sat on either side of me.

I thought of the way
they would be erased
or their bodies blurred

by some news station intern.
How in this picture,
my soft curls are covered

with a beanie to protect
myself from the cold.
My face screwed up

in ironic menace.
When the nightstick
powders my cheekbones,

when the error
of my existence
is a breathless body,

these will be
the pictures they use:
shadows darkening

my skin, hoodie
half-covering my eyes,
beneath my chin
a sideways peace sign.

TO MY CARING AND WORRIED MOTHER:

There are sliced carrots in the shape
of a cowbell because I understand
great food should sing to you.

There's a novel about Alzheimer's
and some magic memory pills for Grandma.

There's an automatic food dispenser
so you don't have to feed the dogs anymore.

There's a travel bag with a Bible
and a plane ticket to Paris.

There's a color-coded flow chart
describing the best way to carry
a conversation with Grandma.

In the bottom right-hand corner,
in fine print, it explains, you may
have to adopt new tactics on the fly.

I caught Grandma watching
The Hulk in Spanish today.
I just flipped to the English version.

To my caring and worried mother:
raising your voice won't help,
there is no cure.

All the Post-it notes
on all the cabinets
should say: *open with caution,*
eat with intensity,

remember,
we love you
and we'll help you
find the watch
you stuffed in the cookie jar.

DÉGRINGOLADE

this slow souring / so dumb / so demented
the body bent / toward a break / the mind
un-mending / a dented / domino effect / affect-
less/ no dominion / over demeanor / dearth
demon / in the tawdry / dome / tamed / to a t
dormant / tenant / in a dungeon / dentured
and denatured / answering / only / to one / demand

SONNET

I hated that faux-urn arrangement:
white, hard plastic, and inescapable
as an abyss. Like all the flawed gods,
you went out in flame and fury.
Studies on your organs must long
be done; did we receive the findings?
Odd to find anything in this much loss.
I'm not gussying it up enough, am I,
dear Reader? There were no blood-curdling
screams, no easy parallels of wilting
dandelions, no family come to Jesus.
The room smelled of shrimp-fried rice
and onion bagels, strawberry cream cheese,
and orange Fanta.

THE COLOSSUS OF MIAMI

Geography is destiny, they say. Geography blessed me with mustard seed barbecue sauce and a smoke-encircled rib shack with a line bending around three blocks. Blessed me with Hellcats and Peaches. Manatees languishing beneath my dangling feet. Here, winter-ripe iguanas freeze and drop stunned from the trees. Here, as there, the eclectic menu of pig parts and cool cups, conch salad, and souse. The halt of traffic for a convoy of crabs. Here, as there, a childhood of water parks and faulty warnings of *fast daughters*. Saga Bay, Perrine, Richmond Heights, Goulds. Goulds sounds like gold, like a gleaming greeting of teeth, like the gliding ride of glistening impalas. I got my jumper from my godmother: a gift I'm reminded of when someone points and yells *shooter* before the game begins. Our first rented home was on Christmas Street, but momma made me promise not to spoil the secret. Remember my father's keloid scars, his exaggerated barrel tip, and speedy arc to the baseball. I pushed the camera closer, ran it over ichor running in the blood of black giants.

WEST PERRINE PARK (THE BIG PARK)

>...it gave these Black men their poetry — Howard Bryant

A white boy asked me to walk him to the bathroom before
a baseball game at a public park where my father was once

pseudonymed myth, he (Eight The Snake), and a generation
of Hellcats (Peewee, Crow, Romie, Termite, and others),

had been good for pockets and bad for business as fans won
ends on the weekend, betting and rooting for the home team—

everyone in their Easter Sunday, straight-from-the-pew,
alabaster best (or home whites), swaying behind home plate

and sprinkled down the right field line like sea foam teasing
the shore—then decided to opt out of the grinding march

of money-making come Monday; what the boy seemed too
afraid to understand, was that all the men crowding around

the teal, worn-metal bleachers behind the dugout, were arguing
about the Dolphins or playing the dozens or sipping grape soda

or rolling bones or narrating the sweat-ballet unfurling atop
the two-toned green and pink-red basketball court—and all

those men would soon be rooting for him because he was
wearing orange and green; what was unseen were the tightened

black backs of the men who built the field he could now
extend his dreams on; I think he homered that day, rounding

the bases with a surprised smile as the Hellcats of old tapered
a fade or faded from memory; he always played better on this

hallowed ground he couldn't divorce from phantom echoes
of bullets and blood. I walked the boy across the second, unused

court to the bathroom, our metal cleats tapping a tune of pregame
buzz and jitters, while a mother weaved box braids into her daughter's

hair down the left field line, and the memories of a Milk Man
with no milk hung like fog in the air around the backstop—

Bubble Gum Stadium, they called it.

UNSENT LETTER TO MY LITTLE COUSIN

Remember when I jacked you up for getting slick with Grandma? I'm sorry. Her brain was dimming and graying like fat on steak. By then, even the advantage of a quip was too much for me to take. I was grieving a long list of losses, those past and those waiting in the futureless distance. I was grieving a blooming grave of language. This was long after I was the dreaming boy, afloat on the untroubled waters of my dreams. I never heard the screams. Your uncle, stabbed on the front porch, and my mother, on her hands and knees, scrubbing blood and history from the faded beige tiles. The same porch where you could find grandma arched over her aloe vera every morning. What to make of the dreaming boy, of his faithfulness to escape. I chased you in circles over the overgrown grass of the backyard after you raised the rim as I was dunking. I could have chipped a tooth or been concussed but wasn't. An only child, I never learned to laugh at myself. Once, in college, I left a stranger's bed to drive you to school. In the moist dark, it was hard to explain. *Who sings this*, you asked. The Weeknd? *Let's keep it that way.* You teach me about the lightness of light. You're a father now. Down deep, was this the plan all along? Is this the only way our people are classic, canonical? Maybe you've got fatherhood licked. You, the seedling, heading for the heavens with four other seedlings, flooding in and out of a small house. Grandma had nine brothers and sisters. She called toddler you *Chuckie* for the dusty morning hue of your hair. You, the additional black Rugrat, left on the cutting room floor. You weren't yet born when I fell headfirst into a glass on the carpeted ground, when doctors and all the loved ones in the room learned, in unison, my spirit was impervious to anesthesia. They had to use a straitjacket to keep me still, to steady my head for the physician's needle and thread. Grandma must have been a light sleeper. When your uncle called out in the middle of the night, she was first to greet him in the flooding grooves between tiles. I suspect, you too, know the splashing call of the dream, the way the waves turn chains to air. I should have stopped in Dallas to visit last summer. What was I afraid of?

SONNET

I got a blowjob once & my grandmother
hated me. It was nearly that simple.
Faux gold watch lost in the damned river
of memory. We had a loose appreciation
of distance & intimacy. Sharing a strawberry
blintz & strong coffee. A claustrophobic red room,
where I fed myself on a dream. Her, in the expanding
claustrophobia of the mind. The only solace
we could offer—soft echo of raindrops
on the surface of the sea. Merciless, drowned
night at the gate of an almost endless sleep.
Resurrection, brief satan-less reprieve,
god's final exam, & finally, paradise.
Momma plans to meet you there.

MOTHER'S VISIT

I loop to & through
domestic arrivals
until the conveyor
belt of baggage
finally frees mother
from its hold.

*This is an interesting
apartment,* she says.

She suggests
a new styling cream,
soap containers,
another towel rack,
& this, all before
diagraming
the moisture
retention of pine.

She forgets
her charger,
she forgets
her toothbrush,
she remembers
an unspoken
half-joke—
I hope the seatbelt
fits around me.

We hope to meet up
with Dan & his father.
We hope to meet up
with Dora & Kyle &
their two kids.

I've been reading
about chosen families
& a crisis of connection.

Mother
alludes to
the God-sized
hole in my life—

my poems,
my poems,
my poems.

They grow
on her
like the
apartment.

button poetry

ACKNOWLEDGMENTS

My sincere thanks to the editors and staff at the following publications for first acknowledging the poems (and previous versions of the poems) in this manuscript:

the Under Review: "West Perrine, Florida"

Into The Void: "House Guests"

The Hopkins Review: "Sonnet" (Pg. 7), "Sonnet" (Pg. 8), "Sonnet" (Pg. 15)

Northern Virginia Review: "Summer"

South Florida Poetry Journal: "Rainbow City"

Nashville Review: "Snuff"

Harpur Palate: "Field Service"

The Cincinnati Review: "Surprise Visit"

The Rush: "F-Stop"

The Florida Review Online: "To My Caring and Worried Mother"

Malarkey Books: "Dégringolade"

Poetry Northwest: "Sonnet" (Pg. 28)

The Adroit Journal: "West Perrine Park (The Big Park)"
Best New Poets: "West Perrine Park (The Big Park)"

RHINO Poetry: "Unsent Letter To My Little Cousin"

Thank you, Sam, Tanesha, Charley, Izzy, and the rest of the Button team for seeing this work and ushering it into the world.

Endless gratitude to my mother who brought me into being and at every turn sacrificed to make my life rich and full of possibilities: I am nothing without you.

Gratitude to my father whose quiet confidence conveyed so many lessons, whose cool permeated even his interest in language, whose interest in language gave birth to my own.

Gratitude to you both for allowing me to dream, for loving me and all my maddening contradictions.

Special thanks to Jaswinder Bolina, my former professor, first poetry mentor, and now friend. You breathed life and confidence into my writing and set me on this journey.

Special thanks to Dora Malech, my second but no less seminal poetry mentor. You know how to care for and teach the whole of the poet; my writing life might not have survived without this. You were and continue to be a safe harbor in unsteady waters.

Gratitude to my teachers aracelis girmay, A. Van Jordan, Amaud Jamaul Johnson, Louise Glück, and Patrick Philips for your support and feedback; to my friends turned family: D.S. Waldman, Christell Victoria Roach, and Dāshaun Washington; and the rest of my Stegner family: Austin Araujo, Jade Cho, Amanda Gunn, Joseph Rios, Adedayo Agarau, Ajibola Tolase, Alison Thumel, Luciana Arbus-Scandiffio, Jackson Holbert, Hua Xi, and Madeleine Cravens.

My words would not be possible without the words and beings of Terrance Hayes, Ross Gay, Hanif Abdurraqib, and Danez Smith.

My thanks to the Robert W. Deutsch Foundation for support which facilitated the writing of some of these poems.

For Glenna, my love and my thank you.

ABOUT THE AUTHOR

Jalen Eutsey was a 2022-2024 Wallace Stegner Fellow at Stanford University. He received his MFA from The Writing Seminars at Johns Hopkins University. He has been the recipient of a Rubys Artist Grant and a Hatty Fitts Walker Scholarship from the Provincetown Fine Arts Work Center. His poems have appeared in *The Yale Review, Best New Poets, Nashville Review,* and *Poetry Northwest.* He was born and raised in Miami.

AUTHOR BOOK RECOMMENDATIONS

Black Movie by Danez Smith

There is much brilliance here. From a subtle turn of phrase like "that odd flood of yes," to making plain the unrelenting nature of American violence and racism, and still managing to land in possibility—"& no one kills the black boy. & no one kills the black boy. & no one kills the black boy." Danez Smith's *Black Movie* offers up dirges and dream songs, shining a light on what racism and fear have wrought, while elevating all the joy, grace, and bond of Black life.

bound by Claire Schwartz

These poems bend and turn like running water, like paths of forced migration. In Claire Schwartz' *bound*, we taste the bittersweet mixture of loving in a world ever under threat, where "a history / distended with myth" leaves no land, no body, no poem, un-haunted.

CREDITS

Assistant Editor
Isabelle Miller

Book Photography
Emily Van Cook

Cover and Interior Design
Victoria Alvarez
Kashia Yang

Distribution
SCB Distributors

Ebook Production
Siva Ram Maganti

Editor
Charley Eatchel

Publisher
Sam Van Cook

Publishing Operations Manager
TaneshaNicole Kozler

Publishing Operations Assistant
Charley Eatchel

Social Media and Marketing
Catherine Guden
Isabelle Miller
Eric Tu

OTHER BOOKS BY BUTTON POETRY

If you enjoyed this book, please consider checking out some of our others, below. Readers like you allow us to keep broadcasting and publishing. Thank you!

Kevin Kantor, *Please Come Off-Book*
Ollie Schminkey, *Dead Dad Jokes*
Reagan Myers, *Afterwards*
L.E. Bowman, *What I Learned From the Trees*
Patrick Roche, *A Socially Acceptable Breakdown*
Rachel Wiley, *Revenge Body*
Ebony Stewart, *BloodFresh*
Ebony Stewart, *Home.Girl.Hood.*
Kyle Tran Myhre, *Not A Lot of Reasons to Sing, but Enough*
Steven Willis, *A Peculiar People*
Topaz Winters, *So, Stranger*
Darius Simpson, *Never Catch Me*
Blythe Baird, *Sweet, Young, & Worried*
Siaara Freeman, *Urbanshee*
Robert Wood Lynn, *How to Maintain Eye Contact*
Junious 'Jay' Ward, *Composition*
Usman Hameedi, *Staying Right Here*
Sean Patrick Mulroy, *Hated for the Gods*
Sierra DeMulder, *Ephemera*
Taylor Mali, *Poetry By Chance*
Matt Coonan, *Toy Gun*
Matt Mason, *Rock Stars*
Miya Coleman, *Cottonmouth*
Ty Chapman, *Tartarus*
Lara Coley, *ex traction*
DeShara Suggs-Joe, *If My Flowers Bloom*
Ollie Schminkey, *Where I Dry the Flowers*
Edythe Rodriguez, *We, the Spirits*
Topaz Winters, *Portrait of My Body as a Crime I'm Still Committing*
Zach Goldberg, *I'd Rather Be Destroyed*
Eric Sirota, *The Rent Eats First*
Neil Hilborn, *About Time*
Josh Tvrdy, *Smut Psalm*
Phil SaintDenisSanchez, *before & after our bodies*
Ebony Stewart, *WASH*
L.E. Bowman, *Shapeshifter*
Najya Williams, *on a date with disappointment*

Available at buttonpoetry.com/shop and more!

BUTTON POETRY BEST SELLERS

Neil Hilborn, *Our Numbered Days*
Hanif Abdurraqib, *The Crown Ain't Worth Much*
Olivia Gatwood, *New American Best Friend*
Sabrina Benaim, *Depression & Other Magic Tricks*
Melissa Lozada-Oliva, *peluda*
Rudy Francisco, *Helium*
Rachel Wiley, *Nothing Is Okay*
Neil Hilborn, *The Future*
Phil Kaye, *Date & Time*
Andrea Gibson, *Lord of the Butterflies*
Blythe Baird, *If My Body Could Speak*
Rudy Francisco, *I'll Fly Away*
Andrea Gibson, *You Better Be Lightning*
Rudy Francisco, *Excuse Me As I Kiss The Sky*

Available at buttonpoetry.com/shop and more!

◆